EYE-LOOK
Picture Games

Alike or Not Alike?

A Photo Sorting Game

by Kristen McCurry

CAPSTONE PRESS
a capstone imprint

A+ books are published by Capstone Press,
1710 Roe Crest Drive, North Mankato, Minnesota 56003.
www.capstonepub.com

Books published by Capstone Press are manufactured with paper containing at least 10 percent post-consumer waste.

Library of Congress Cataloging-in-Publication Data
McCurry, Kristen.
 Alike or not alike? : a photo sorting game / by Kristen McCurry.
   p. cm.—(A+ books. eye-look picture games)
 Includes bibliographical references.
 Summary: "Simple text invites readers to sort groups of objects in full-color photos"—Provided by publisher.
 ISBN 978-1-4296-7549-9 (library binding)
 1. Picture puzzles—Juvenile literature. I. Title. II. Series.

 GV1507.P47M374 2012
 793.73—dc23   2011043258

Credits
Jeni Wittrock, editor; Tracy Davies McCabe, designer; Marcie Spence, media researcher; Sarah Schuette, photo stylist, Marcy Morin, studio scheduler

Photo Credits
Capstone Studio: Karon Dubke, 4 (top right and bottom left), 5 (top left), 7 (bottom right), 9 (top right and bottom right), 10, 11 (all), 12, 13 (all), 14, 17 (top right), 18, 19 (bottom both), 21 (top right), 23 (bottom left), 25 (top left and bottom left), 27 (all), 28, 29, 30-31; Shutterstock: Ann Cantelow 21 (bottom left), Anne Kitzman, 5 (bottom right), atoss, 3 (left), BARRI, 23 (bottom right), 24, Bruno Ferrari, 23 (top right), Cameramannz, 15 (top right), Emin Ozkan, 9 (top left), Gina Smith, 21 (bottom right), 22, Ian D Walker, 3 (right), 4 (middle left), 17 (bottom left), Ivonne Wierink, cover (top left), Iwona Grodzka, cover (bottom right), James Coleman, 4 (middle right), 19 (top left), Jennifer Stone, 7 (top right), 8, Jerry Hobert, 4 (bottom right), 15 (bottom right), John Brueske, 17 (bottom right), kavee, 5 (top right), Maksymilian Skolik, 19 (top right), 20, marilyn barbone, 4 (top left), 7 (bottom left), mikeledray, 15 (top left), 16, Mountain Light Studios, 21 (top left), Peter Betts, 7 (top left), pistolseven, 25 (bottom right), 26, pixel-pets cover (bottom left), risteski goce, 17 (top left), Scott Latham, 5 (bottom left), 6, Steve Degenhardt, 25 (top right), Thomas M Perkins, 9 (bottom left), Tischenko Irina, cover (top right), Vitaly Titov & Maria Sidelnikova, 23 (top left)

Note to Parents, Teachers, and Librarians
The Eye-Look Picture Games series supports national math standards related to grouping and sorting and national language arts standards related to the use of comparisons and analogies. The images support early readers in understanding the text. The repetition of words and phrases helps early readers learn new words. Early readers may need assistance to read some words and to use the Read More and Internet Sites sections of the book.

Printed in the United States of America in North Mankato, Minnesota.
102011   006405CGS12

Grouping and Sorting

People group things together that are alike. Alike things are the same in some way. But they may not be the same in every way.

An orange and a beach ball are similar because they are round. A banana and an apple look very different, but they're alike in that they're both delicious fruits. Being round or being food are two examples of ways things can be alike.

This book is full of sorting games. Each game shows four objects. One of them doesn't belong. Can you find the one that's not alike?

Turn each page to check if you are right. **Watch out!** Finding the not-alikes can be trickier than it looks. Want to give it a try?

Which is not alike?

shoes

hat

bicycle

mittens

bicycle

Not Alike

The bicycle is not alike. Why not?
The other pictures show things that
you wear. You can't wear a bicycle!

6

Which is not alike?

elephant

marble

oak tree

semitruck

marble

Not Alike

Why is the marble not alike? Look at its size. A marble is small. The other things are all big.

Which is not alike?

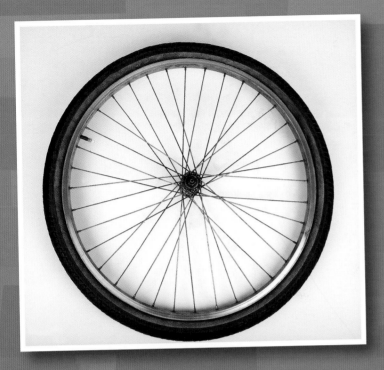

bicycle tire

clock face

tambourine

yield sign

yield sign

Not Alike

One of these shapes doesn't belong!
The yield sign is a triangle. Look *around*
at the others. They're all circles!

Which is not alike?

rock

dog

goldfish

flower

rock

Not Alike

What makes the rock different? A fish, a flower, and a dog are all living things. A rock is not living.

Which is not alike?

scissors

hammer

shoes

spoon

shoes

Not Alike

Hands are handy. You use a scissors, hammer, and spoon with your hands. But not shoes.

Which is not alike?

wagon

strawberry

ice pop

apple

wagon

Not Alike

All of these things are red. What makes
the wagon different? Even if you are
very hungry, you can't eat a wagon.

Which is not alike?

teddy bear

scissors

beach ball

marble

scissors

Not Alike

Did you choose the scissors? Why? You can play with a doll, a ball, or a marble. But scissors are not a toy.

Which is not alike?

skunk

roses

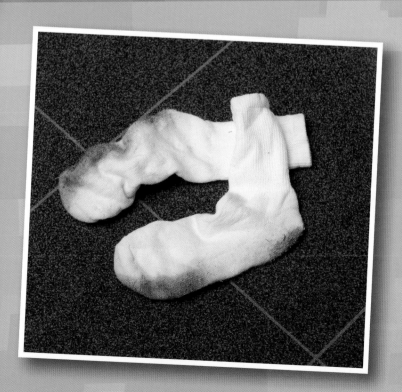

dirty socks

garbage can

roses

Not Alike

Roses smell nice. But the other three are stinky. P.U.!

Which is not alike?

scooter

wagon

bicycle

sled

sled

Not Alike

You ride all of these things. But what makes the sled different? The others roll on wheels. A sled just slides!

Which is not alike?

dog

door

doll

carrot

carrot

Not Alike

Why doesn't the carrot belong?
It doesn't start with "d," like dog,
door, and doll do.

Which is not alike?

pizza

hot cocoa

soup

shake

shake

Not Alike

These are all things you can eat.
But three are steaming hot and one
is not. The milkshake is ice cold. Brrr!

Which is not alike?

a sandwich

a pizza

an apple

a pie

a pie

Not Alike

You can eat these things. But the other foods are missing half. This pie is not alike, because you get to eat the whole thing!

You did it! You found the not-alikes. You looked at size, shape, color, and many other things. You had to ask yourself which pictures went together and why. That makes you a super sorting champ!

Read More

Kalman, Bobbie. *Is It the Same or Different?* Looking at Nature. New York: Crabtree, 2008.

Peppas, Lynn. *Sorting.* My Path to Math. New York: Crabtree Pub., 2010.

Steffora, Tracey. *Sorting at the Market.* Math around Us. Chicago: Heinemann Library, 2011.

Internet Sites

FactHound offers a safe, fun way to find Internet sites related to this book. All of the sites on FactHound have been researched by our staff.

Here's all you do:

Visit www.facthound.com

Type in this code: 9781429675499

 Super-cool stuff! Check out projects, games and lots more at www.capstonekids.com